This book Belong to:

....

....

....

TIGER

DOLPHIN

COW

CAT

HIPPOPOTAMUS

HORSE

SQUID

TURTLE

BUFFALO

STARFISH

SHARK

LION

JELLYFISH

KOALA

RABBIT

My Favorite Book

Directions: Draw the cover of your favorite book and write a sentence about it below

TREE

Carrot

Eggplant

Flower

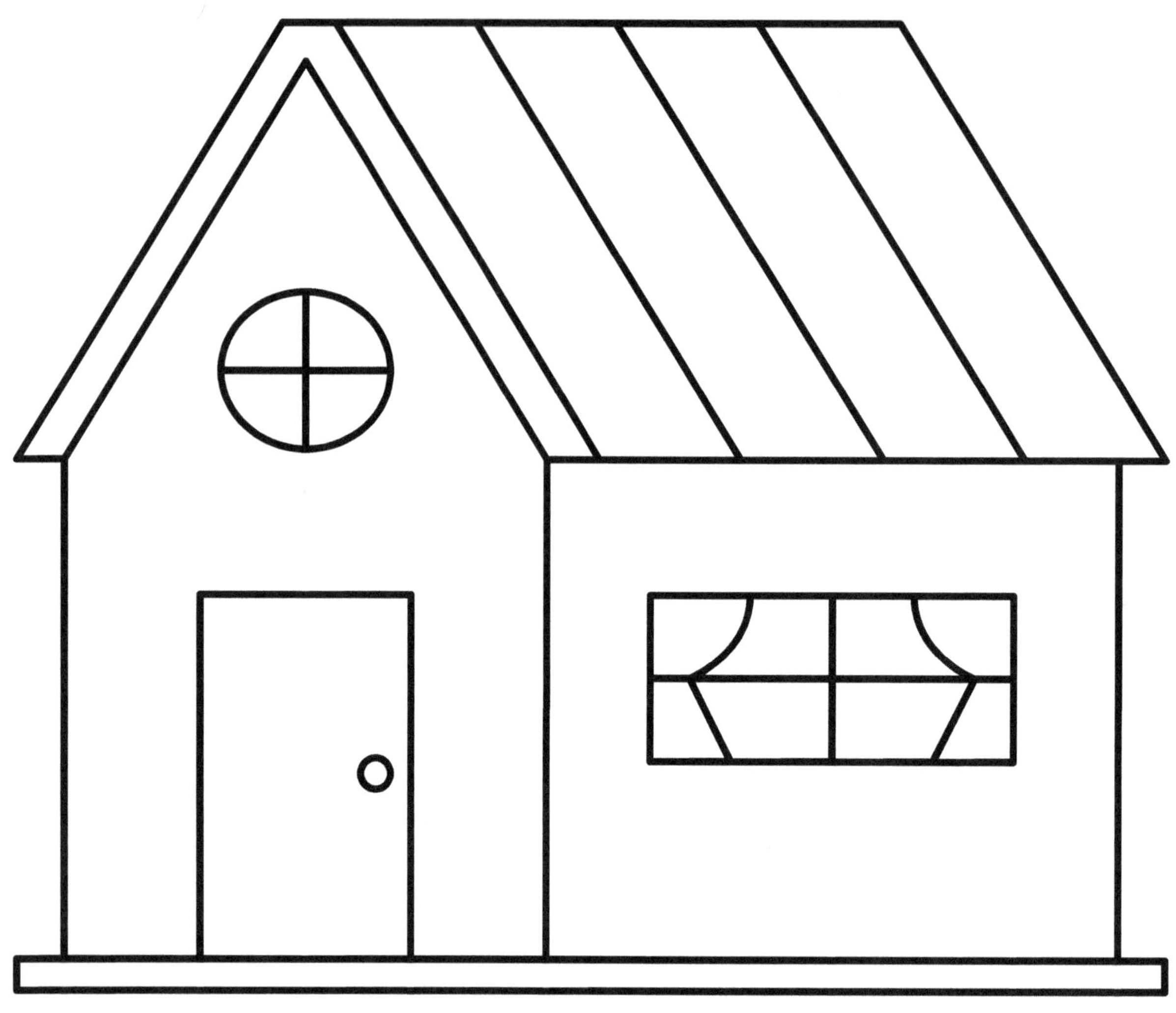

House

Light Bulb

Mango

Notepad

Orange

Pinwheel

Rose

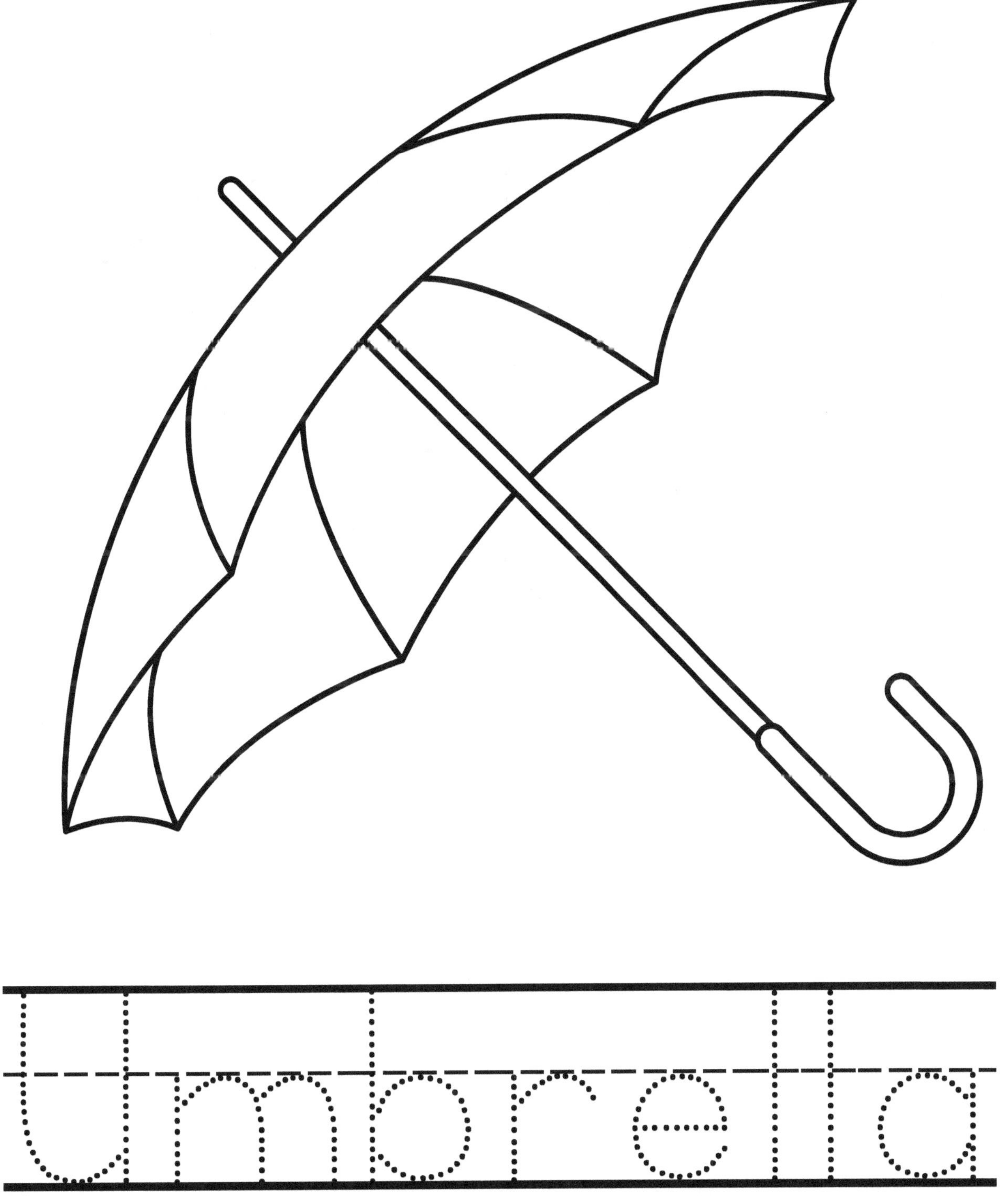

Umbrella

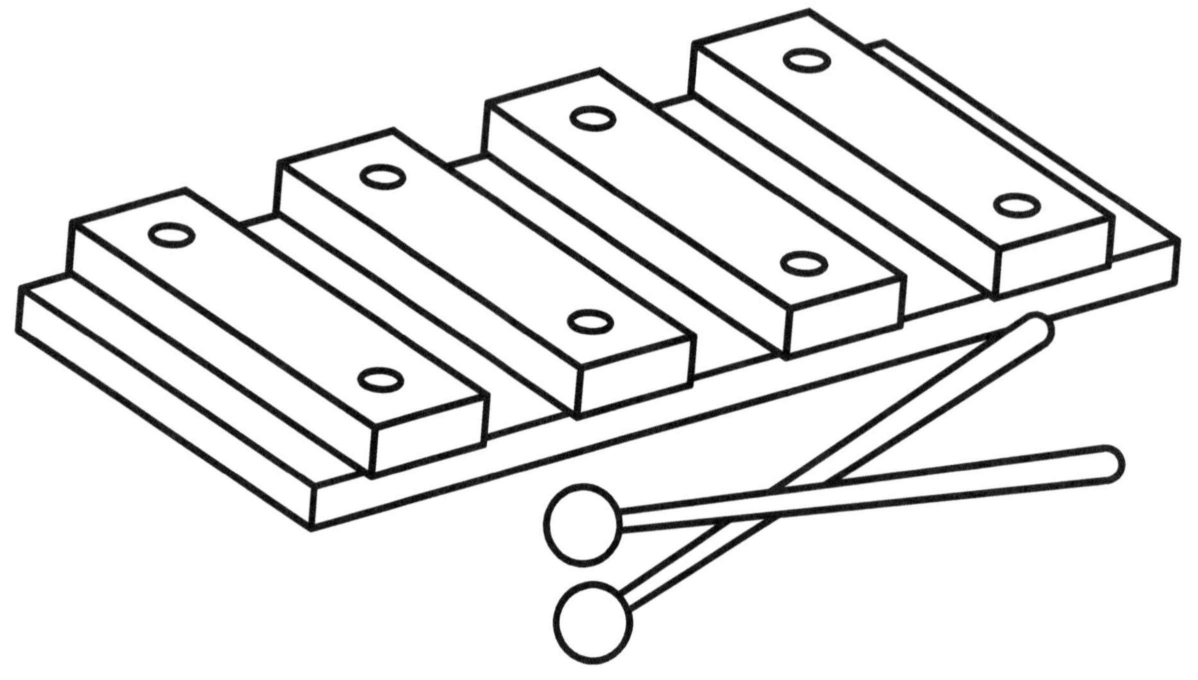

Xylophone

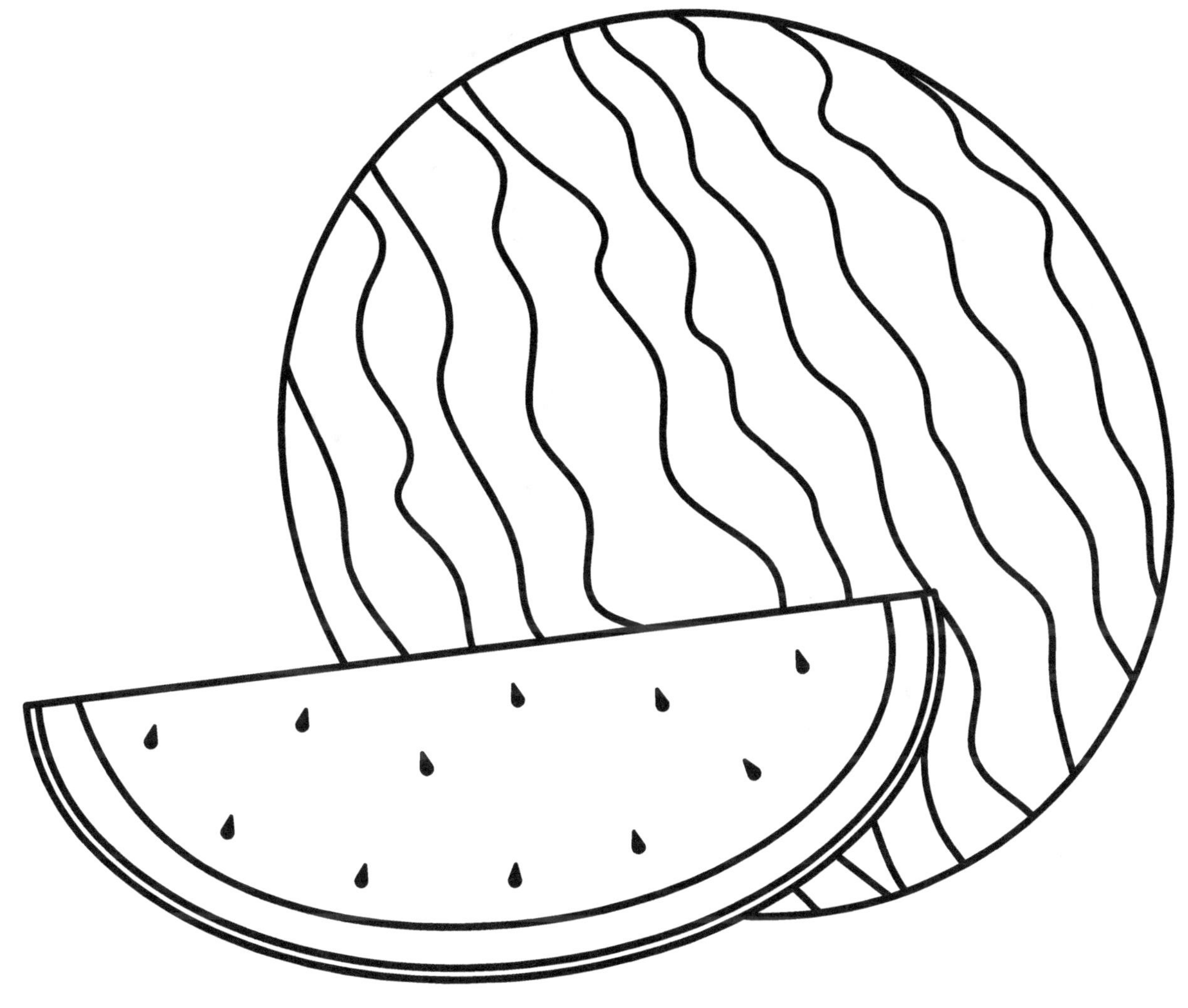

Watermelon

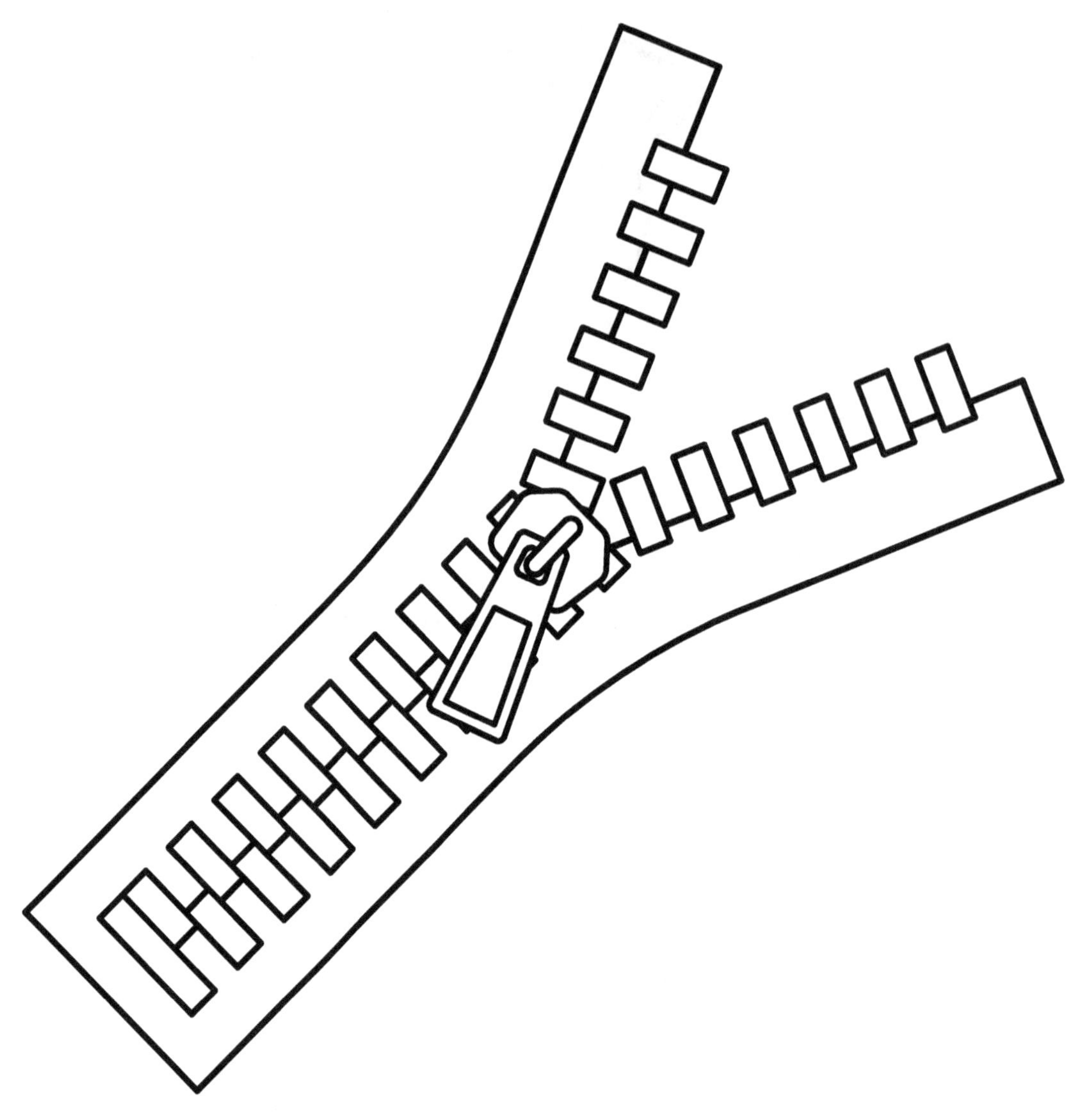

Zipper

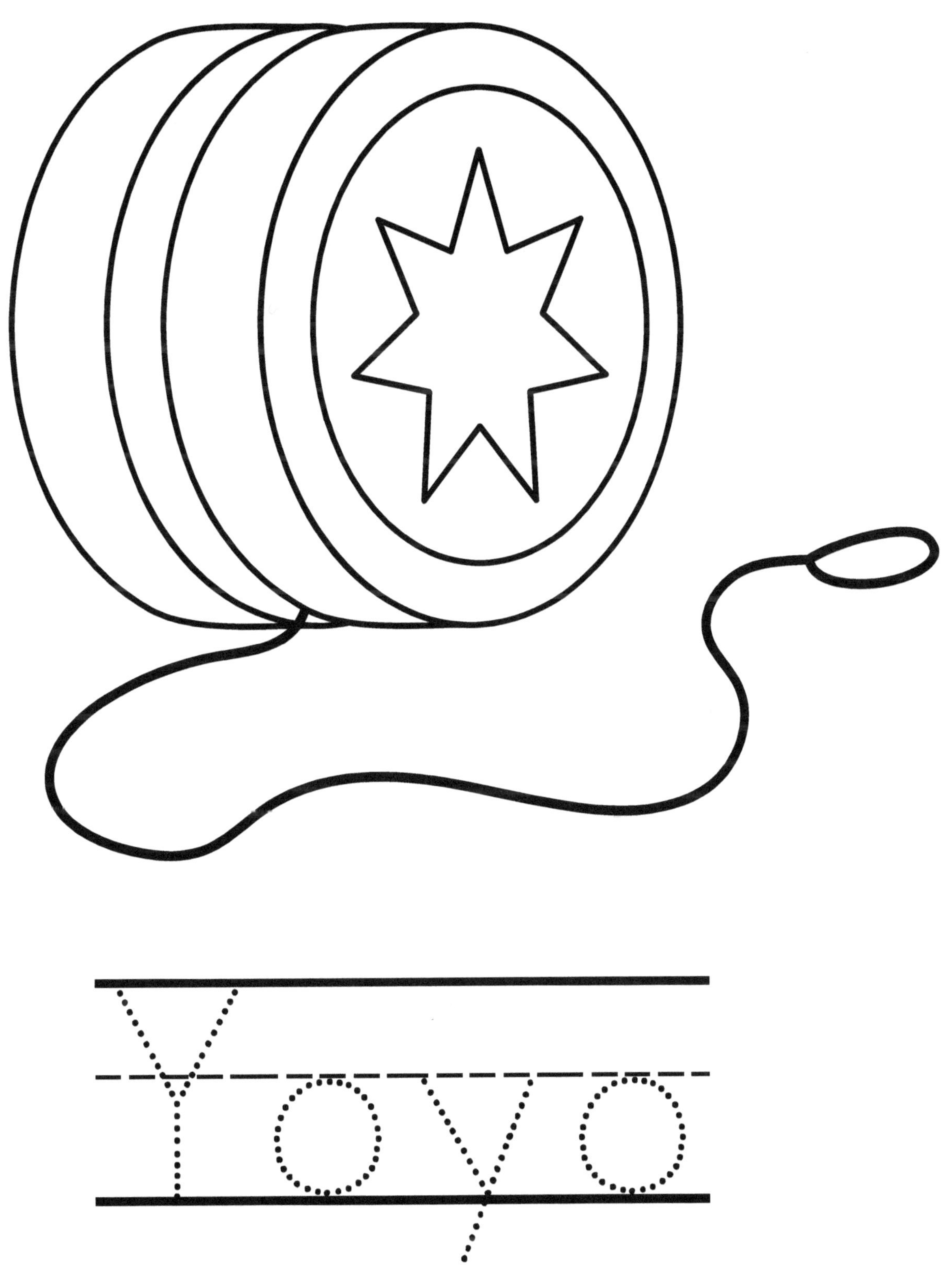
Yoyo

www.ingramcontent.com/pod-product-compliance
Lightning Source LLC
LaVergne TN
LVHW080559160826
845677LV00010B/1917
* 9 7 9 8 3 5 2 1 3 6 0 1 0 *